More Airs for
Arranged by
Matt Seattle

Introduction

Like its companion, AIRS FOR PAIRS, this book contains twenty-one tunes from Britain and Ireland. The first book contains some of the most popular traditional tunes which, the editor feels, should have a place in the repertoire of all musicians who reside in these islands, whatever their chosen specialisation. This second book contains more of this core repertoire, but also has some interesting older tunes as well as some more recent music composed in traditional idioms. The balance here is weighted a little more in favour of the slower tunes - for no particular reason. As in the first book the harmonies have been written not to be easy or difficult, but to be musical. I would like to thank Stewart Hardy for playing them all through with me and making many valuable suggestions which I have been pleased to include.

Suggested bowings are included in the arrangements. These will work perfectly well, but there are of course other possibilities, and personal familiarity with one or another of the native idioms is always a better guide than written instructions. The music is playable on instruments other than violin, and some of the tunes derive specifically from piping and harping, as well as fiddling traditions.

It is possible that more volumes in the series will appear in due course, and I am happy to receive comments about the present books and suggestions for future additions to the series. There is no reason to play harmonies to traditional tunes other than enjoyment of the result, and if any enjoyment results from the use of these duets, then the arranger will be more than repaid for his time.

More Airs for Pairs   **Compiled and arranged by Matt Seattle**

Tune arrangements, harmonies and text copyright © 2006 Matt Seattle (MCPS, PRS)

ISBN 1 899512 71 3

A catalogue in print record for this title is available from the British Library.

Acknowledgements

Cover design: Bruce Baillie 01274 693475

Original cover artwork and artwork this page: David Hall, Briar Rose Studio

Printed by Fretwell Print & Design Limited, Keighley, 01535 600714

Originally a Dragonfly Music Publication

Now produced and published by

mally.com

3 East View , Moorside, Cleckheaton, West Yorkshire, BD19 6LD, U.K.

Tel: +44 (0)1274 876388   Fax: +44 (0)1274 865208

Email: mally@mally.com   Web: http://www.mally.com

Copyright © 2006 mally

A mally production

1. Banish Misfortune

Two Irish jigs: **Banish Misfortune** is a good invocation at the start of a music session, and many sessions actually begin with the tune, an Irish pipers' favourite. The harmony is mainly built on contrary motion - the fortunes of the two players rise and fall, coming together at the end. You might like to try a continuous or rhythmic drone accompaniment for contrast. The tune is also known as *The Humours of Mullinafauna* and **The Blackthorn Stick** is also known as *The Humours of Bantry*.

Irish Piper.

2. The Blackthorn Stick

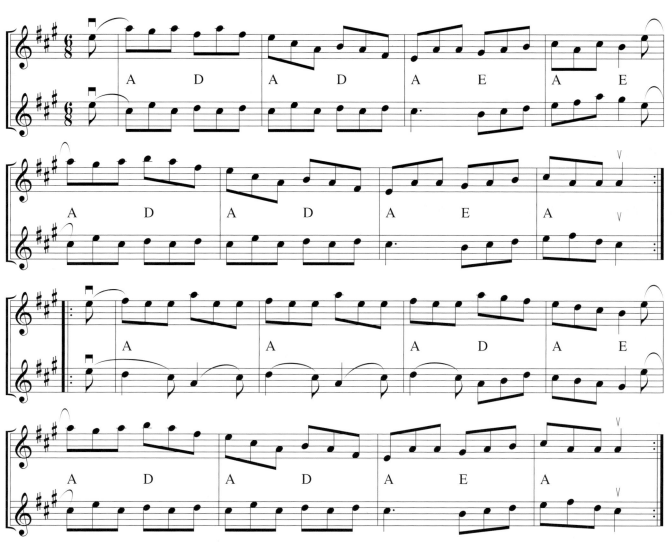

3. Nonesuch

Nonesuch and **Portsmouth** were both published in editions of John Playford's Dancing Master (1651 and 1701 respectively). Nonesuch was actually published in minor and major versions in different editions of the book, and both work well. This tune also sounds good with a drone accompaniment, and was perhaps an old English bagpipe tune (it is certainly one today, as can be heard from the ensemble pictured on the right, **The Goodacre Brothers English Bagpipe Trio**). Portsmouth, possibly an old hornpipe dance tune, has been in the Top Twenty in living memory in a version by Mike Oldfield.

4. Portsmouth

5. The Hens' March

The Hens' March is possibly the most difficult tune in this book, and it is a real fiddler's party piece. It was published in duet form in Scotland by Robert Bremner around 1760 and later by Peter Milne in 1870. It was revived by Tom Anderson, the leading light of Shetland fiddling in the 20th century, and given another boost by English fiddler Dave Swarbrick. No two versions, including mine, are quite the same as each other, but I have borrowed from Robert Bremner the "clucking in canon" in the second section.

A confident and vigorous approach to bowing is needed here, with the ability to recover smartly between consecutive down-bows. Try ringing the open A string along with the melody in places (e.g. line 1 bar 2; line 2 bar 1). The second fiddler needs to keep time carefully in the clucking section, where the small clashes of harmony between the parts shouldn't be too conspicuous amid the general clamour.

6. *The Banks of the Tyne*

T Murray

The Banks of the Tyne is a simple but lovely waltz tune discovered in the manuscript collection of Jack Armstrong, celebrated Northumbrian piper, fiddler and bandleader. The identity of the composer, T Murray, remains a mystery at present.

More Airs for Pairs

7. The Boys Of Bluehill

Two hornpipes: **The Boys of Bluehill** and **Off to California** are probably Irish in origin, but played widely elsewhere. The first is also known as *The Beaux of Oakhill* and *The Lads of North Tyne*, and it is given here with Newcastle bowing, where the bow strokes mainly tie notes across the beat to produce a swinging effect. The dotted rhythm is used by general agreement in writing out "lilting" hornpipes, but the dotted quaver and semiquaver pairs are usually played as crotchet-quaver triplets, and this has been taken into account in writing the harmonies.

More Airs for Pairs

8. Off to California

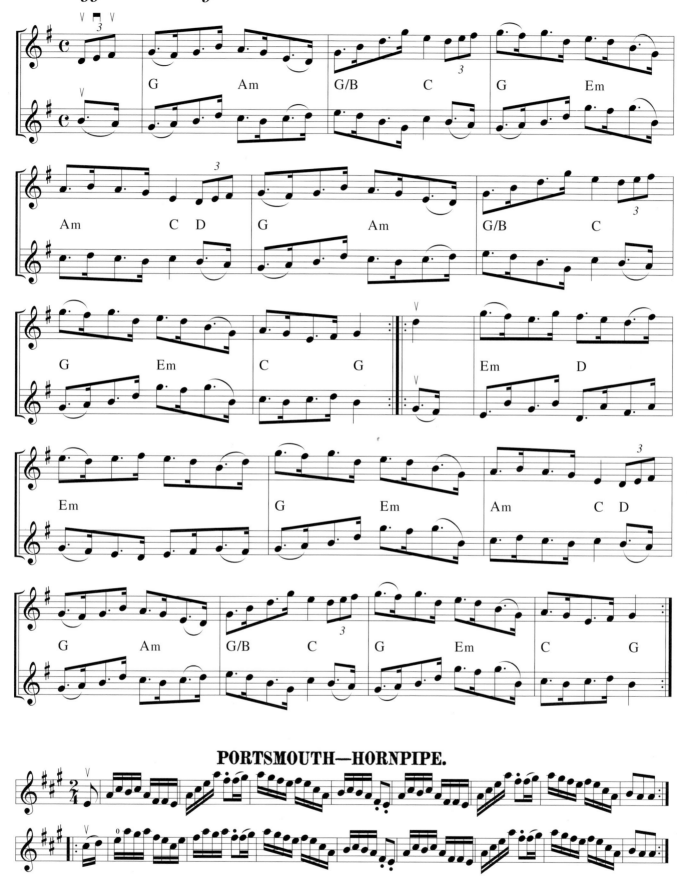

PORTSMOUTH—HORNPIPE.

This version of the tune from the 19th century American publication, Ryan's Mammoth Collection, illustrates how a tune can change its title, its key, its rhythm and many of its notes without losing its identity. Strangely, it also has the same title as a completely different tune in this book.

9. The Hesleyside Reel

T J Elliott

10. The Flowers of Edinburgh

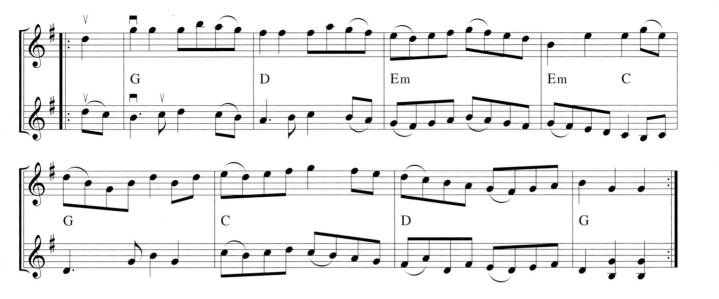

11. The Dinnington Rant

T Murray

The Hesleyside Reel is a modern Northumbrian tune and a smallpipers' favourite.

The Flowers of Edinburgh is a well known reel which first appeared in the 18th century, when it was described as a Scots Measure.

The Dinnington Rant comes from the same source as *The Banks of the Tyne*.

12. Enrico

13. Danny Boy

Enrico is a tune of unknown origin - one older published version is from Ireland - but it has become popular among English fiddlers through its inclusion in the manuscript music collection of Thomas Hardy the novelist, poet and fiddler. Hardy's version also had the title *Jacob*, and a version in a Sussex manuscript is called *Water Loo Fair* or *The Henryco*.

Danny Boy, probably the most famous Irish song air, needs no introduction.

14. The Hole in the Wall

15. The Bishop of Bangor's Jig

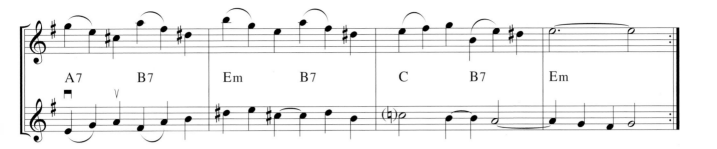

16. The Roving Pedlar

The Hole in the Wall and **The Bishop of Bangor's Jig** both come from Playford's Dancing Master (first published 1698 and 1701 respectively). The Bishop has naturally been claimed as Welsh, and Henry Purcell is said to have composed The Hole in the Wall.

The Roving Pedlar is an Irish air published in the 19th century in one of O'Farrell's books for Irish pipes. The ABBA form and unusual five-bar phrases are found in several older Irish tunes.

17. Carolan's Draught
Turlough O'Carolan

Carolan's Draught is one of the most popular compositions of the Irish harper Turlough O'Carolan (1670 - 1738). Its title suggests the composer was fond of a drink or two, a predilection which may produce the tendency to **Sleep Soond ida Moarnin** (sleep sound in the morning). The second strain of this fine Shetland reel has a good example of the bowing pattern known in the USA as the Georgia Shuffle: accenting the single down-bow among the slurred up-bows gives a strong off-beat effect which is also heard in much Irish fiddling.

More Airs for Pairs

18. Sleep Soond ida Moarnin

19. Lindisfarne

Matt Seattle

Lindisfarne was composed in 1990 and is named after the island rather than the drink or the band. It won first prize in the Rothbury Traditional Music Festival original tune competition in the same year. The winner in 1993 was **Elizabeth's Waltz**, named after the composer's daughter.

20. Elizabeth's Waltz
Kim Bibby-Wilson

** Variations on these two bars on the repeat of the second strain:

First time through tune

Second time through tune

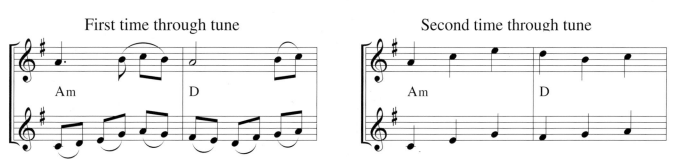

21. Farewell to Whisky

Niel Gow

Farewell to Whisky was composed by Niel Gow, the most celebrated Scottish fiddler of the 18th century. The original published version (written with note values half the duration of those here) contains the direction "Very Slow and Pathetick" and the explanation: "This tune alludes to prohibiting the making of Whisky in 1799. It is expressive of a Highlander's sorrow on being deprived of his Favorite Beverage." The law in question was repealed in 1801 but the tune has remained popular ever since.